Power To Pray

Copyright © 2013 by Nancy Andreson

All rights reserved. No part of this publication may be reproduced, stored in a retrieval system, or transmitted by any means – electronic, mechanical, photographic (photocopying), recording, or otherwise – without prior permission in writing from the author.

Printed in the United States of America
ISBN: 9781482501018

Learn more information at:
www.thevineyardchurch.tv

Contents

CHAPTER ONE ~ Our Name is House of Prayer

CHAPTER TWO ~ When Shall I Pray?

CHAPTER THREE ~ Prayer is Work

CHAPTER FOUR ~ Authority To Pray For Nations

CHAPTER FOUR ½ ~ Or Are We Just Kidding Ourselves?

CHAPTER FIVE ~ Why Prayer?

CHAPTER SIX ~ Where Should We Pray?

CHAPTER SEVEN ~ Our Prayer and the Helper

CHAPTER EIGHT ~ The Rule of Wrestling

CHAPTER NINE ~ The Throne and The Lamb

CHAPTER TEN ~ Praying That Works

ACKNOWLEDGMENTS

I have had many wonderful years of growing in my experience of God by studying His word with other women. Along the way many have encouraged me to write a bible study book on my own—a task which seemed hugely daunting. I'd particularly like to thank Maura Glynn, my daughter, Tamar Allen, Mary Garner, and Jeanne Costello for their continuing persistence and encouragement. While this isn't a "bible study", their confidence in me provided me the courage to attempt this project.

I would also like to thank my husband Don for standing behind me. He kept telling me I'd do a great job writing his study guide. My goal was to help make his book, "Power to Pray", a working book for use in small groups (this was after a number of people who read the book asked him to do a workbook to go along with this). When Vineyard Resources encouraged him to do the same, we figured we should take this as a Word from God and create this study guide as an added resource.

It has been fun, rich, as well as a privilege to be Don's wife and partner for 44 years. I think if a book were to be written of all of the great romances in time our names would surely be found in one of its many chapters. Having lived many of Don's experiences in prayer you get the added insights of the wife!

Many thanks go to our long-term friend, Lois Kernan, who did the layout for this project. She and I have worked together for years on many written and visual projects. She has an incredible eye and gift for taking a project from the typed word or visual images I've sent along and making them into something that is visually striking and carries impact just through her gift of presentation. She has been a wonderful sounding board and editor for my ideas. I consider her an equal partner in pulling together some very wonderful projects for the King.

Thanks Be to God! I consulted and depended on His directions for every step of this little project. I'm not blaming Him for the book's weaknesses. Those can be squarely left on my doorstep! God and I had many ongoing conversations as I wrote. It was a crazy challenge to try and create something that could enhance this book, as I believe it is so well written!

Don has done an incredible job in making his book readable — thorough and deep. I trust and hope this study/discussion guide will be a great additional voice, which will help you touch and lay hold of the truths Don has written about. As I wrote it I was praying that it might make the book more usable — like a lump of soft clay it would become something you can hold, mold and stick your fingers, mind and imagination into and that it will spark some great conversations with God and others. If that happens then I will feel that God has answered my prayers!

HOW TO USE THIS BOOK

This Study Guide is meant to be used as a companion book to "Power to Pray". You will get greater benefit from the material if you work through the guide one chapter at a time, immediately after finishing the chapter with the same title. It was designed for use by a small group, but can also be done independently.

Power To Pray

Study/Discussion Guide

"My Father's house shall be called a house of prayer for all the nations." Mark 11:15

Chapter One
Our Name is House of Prayer

Briefly describe your experience of prayer.

Use a word picture, write a poem, or draw a real picture of a house (you can include the yard), or a pie chart that you feel would most represent all aspects of your relationship with God—worship, service, giving, church, prayer, study, outreach, etc. If you are meeting with a group later, share your pictures and writings.

> *"I pray because of what I believe the results will be, not because of what happens to me every time I pray."*
> *Pg. 1*

Had you ever thought of your life as a House of Prayer?

How does it make you feel?

Are you content with the portion that prayer represents in your word or picture drawing?

If you are, great! Take time to share your experience of prayer with the group. If you are not satisfied (be honest), what do you like least about praying? Share with the group.

Think of some reasons why God doesn't make prayer a spiritual high each and every time you engage with Him.

What do you consider a good reason to pray?

Are there attitudes you need to change to embrace growing in your conversations with God?

PRAYER ACTION STEP

ON YOUR OWN . . .

Take time to say a prayer similar to this one. (It might be helpful to write it down and date it. You could even place a copy in your bible).

"Lord this is where I am today. (Fill in the blank and include your current unhelpful attitudes). And I see it is not what you desire for me. I know what you want to do in me and what you even promise to do in me! Even though I don't feel like I want it, I am willing. Would you empower my heart to change and to become a more effective partner in order to help bring Your Kingdom to the world around me. I want to be included with those about whom you boast saying, 'They are my House of Prayer'".

"The faith Jesus described is faith in a Person, not a force.

True faith that moves mountains or withers a fig tree is Person-al faith."

Pg. 6

Power To Pray

Study/Discussion Guide

"The earnest prayer of a righteous person has great power and produces wonderful results." James 5:16b.

Chapter Two
When Shall I Pray?

> *"To minister in prayer simply means to serve God by praying."*
> *Pg. 19*

Don emphasizes that there is a difference between the "Ministry OF Prayer" and "Ministry IN Prayer". In your own words describe the difference.

Does this difference help you gain perspective on your own life of prayer? Why or why not?

What four things do we learn by serving God in prayer?   (Pg. 19, Paragraph 6)

    1.

    2.

    3.

    4.

Which of these things is a current growing edge for you?

Had you considered prayer a tool of learning in your growth process?

> *"Partnership learning can happen because when we are praying, we are disciplining ourselves to focus on God."*
> **Pg. 19**

> *"But Lord, I thought your power is available to anyone who asks at any time."*
>
> ***And He answers** "Yes, it is, but there is something larger I am working on. It is an eternal partnership with my people."*
>
> **Pg. 20**

List the three *"When to Pray"* times".

1.

  (Mark 9: 14-29 and John 11:41-42)

2.

  (James 4:2 and James 5:13)

3.

  (Ephesians. 6:18)

Which one of these three "When to Pray" times do you find easiest?

Why?

Which is most challenging for you?

Why?

Read Acts 19:13-16
In context with this chapter on *"When to Pray"* consider and discuss what may be some reasons the demon replied to the sons of Sceva; *"I know Jesus and I know Paul, but who are you?"*

> *"I have found it surprisingly against the grain to pray about that need immediately."*
> **Pg. 21**

Read Acts 4:13
How might this passage apply to your life today?

REFLECTION QUESTION:
What power do we lack because we don't pray at all times — before, during and after?

Do you believe God is ready to partner with you through prayer to see His love and purposes released in impossible situations? If not, why?

PRAYER ACTION STEP

ON YOUR OWN...

As you consider your life right now, is there a "kairos (decisive, God-appointed) moment" you might pray through?

Take time to pray right now.

If not, and your next kairos moment is ahead, what attitudes or adjustments in your life might you commit to God now—believing that when a "kairos moment" arrives you will handle it differently?

Make that your prayer action step.

Power To Pray

Study/Discussion Guide

"The greatest weariness comes from work not done."
Eric Hoffer

Chapter Three
Prayer is Work!

Do you find viewing "prayer as work" helpful?

Why or why not?

Read I Tim.2:1-8. According to Paul how important is prayer to both the quality of life and the salvation of all people?

> *"...here is the truth about what we are doing when we pray: we are laboring the kind of labor that is striving.*
>
> *Simply put, prayer is work—hard work."*
> *Pg. 31*

Discuss or write your thoughts about the relationship of prayer and salvation, and why it might be something targeted by the enemy—or so against our natural desires.

Paul writes *"I have been chosen as a preacher and apostle to teach the Gentiles this message about faith and truth…". (verse 7)*

What connections do you see between faith, truth and prayer?

In this chapter Don talks about the transformation of the disciples' lives. They were disciples who lived with and observed close up how Jesus lived and operated out of prayer. Before his death the disciples don't pray much; yet their lives were transformed into devotion to prayer after His death and resurrection. Don makes this observation: that their lives were transformed into pray-ers as they became disciples who took responsibility for bringing God's Kingdom on their own shoulders.

Read Mark 16:15-20. As a disciple of Jesus reflect on how you view the bringing of God's kingdom. Is it more as an observer of who God is and how he does His job, or do you take the responsibility of bringing the Kingdom in the earth as your own job description?

How might this view affect your devotion to prayer?

Why do you think it affected the prayer life of the disciples?

How have you approached prayer . . .
>   . . . as a skill you can learn?

>   . . . or as something you must be naturally good at?

Share two things you find encouraging about prayer being a skill you can learn.

1.

2.

"The work of prayer requires learning the skills of prayer – and anyone can learn them and keep learning them better, even me."
Pg. 32

> *"I need to view prayer not as a sprint but a marathon."*
> **Pg. 33**

"As a marathoner I can learn to pray with steadiness and 'relaxed determination' knowing I can wait for prayer to unfold as I (or we together) do the work of praying."

Pg. 33

Imagine you are a Webster Dictionary. Write your definitions of:

"relaxed determination"

"prayer unfolding"

Using the 10,000-Hour Rule as a guide (Malcome Gladwell's book, *"Outliers — The Story of Success"*, which says it takes 10,000 hours of practice to become really, really good at something), where would you place yourself on an "established expert" scale as a pray-er?

Do you find this encouraging or discouraging?

Why?

PRAYER ACTION STEP

ON YOUR OWN...

Growing in prayer is a process that happens over a lifetime.

What adjustments would you need to make to prioritize your schedule to make more time to grow your life of prayer?

Take time to commit these to God and ask for his help to follow through.

Most successful changes in life are done in small steps rather than huge leaps.

Feel free to commit these things on paper.

Power To Pray

Study/Discussion Guide

"But God is so rich in mercy, and He loved us so much that even though we were dead because of our sins, He gave us life when He raised Christ from the dead."
Ephesians 2:4

Chapter Four
Authority to Pray for Nations

Describe in a few sentences your attitude and feelings when you are praying for:

1. Personal needs –

2. Nations –

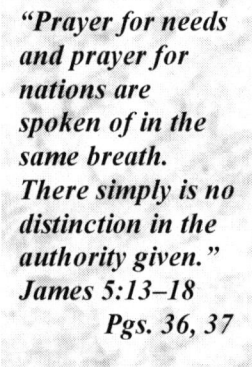

"Prayer for needs and prayer for nations are spoken of in the same breath. There simply is no distinction in the authority given."
James 5:13–18
Pgs. 36, 37

SEVEN TESTS

In this chapter Don lists seven tests each of us must face in our journey as a disciple of Jesus (Pgs. 40-42). Review them in your book. Share which ones you feel you've passed through at least once. (Some may come around more than once.)

Which have been most challenging?

What fear did they unearth in you?

How did you overcome that fear?

Are you in the midst of a test now that you would like prayer for?

Take time in your group to share and pray for one another. If you aren't in a group make a time to get together with someone you trust, and have them PRAY with you.

THREE CHOICES

When considering praying for nations—nations are simply groups of people—Don says we are presented the same three options that Abraham (and others) had:

1. To stand on the side of judgment.
2. To say nothing or opt out of prayer.
3. To assume the responsibility and act in the authority that God's promise has conferred upon us and use it to pray for mercy.

As honestly as possible, which option is most attractive to you when you are facing the choice to pray for the people/nations that you don't like or don't agree with?

> *"I have always found mercy bears richer fruit than strict justice."*
>
> **Abraham Lincoln**

PRAYER ACTION STEP

ON YOUR OWN...

Pick a nation that isn't your favorite nation. If you have a computer, take time to go online to Google news or another news site or go to www.operationworld.org. to get an idea of what is currently going on there. This will add content to your prayers.

Take some time to pray for that nation. Begin your prayer by asking God to give you His heart for this people or place.

Power To Pray

Study/Discussion Guide

"Teach me your ways, O Lord, that I may live according to your truth! Grant me purity of heart so that I may honor you." Psalm 86:11

Chapter 4 ½
Or Are We Just Kidding Ourselves?

Have you ever unexpectedly been interrupted by an urgent sense you needed to pray for something or someone?

Share that experience and include any follow-up results to the experience.

"God is not all or nothing. His plans are not all or nothing. And our prayers are not all or nothing." (Pg. 58 Paragraph 3)

Do you agree or disagree with this statement, and if so, why?

Does this change your attitude about how you approach prayer?

> INCREASING THE EFFECTIVENESS OF OUR PRAYERS BY LIVING IN HARMONY WITH THE WAYS OF GOD.

Look up and rewrite in your own words:

Psalm 40:8

"One of the major factors in the effectiveness of our prayers is the condition of our hearts."
Pg. 58

John 5:30

"God detests the prayers of a person who ignores the law."
Proverbs 28:9

What does it mean to you "to live in harmony with the heart of God"?

On a scale of *one* to *ten* — if one is living totally out of harmony with God's heart, and ten is living your life like Jesus — totally in harmony with God's heart — where would you place your score?

Is this score better, worse, or about the same as a year ago?

Why?

"We know only too well that what we are doing is nothing more than a drop in the ocean.

But if the drop were not there the ocean would be missing something."

Mother Teresa

Do you feel your prayers are more or less effective than one year ago?

How about three years ago?

> INCREASING THE EFFECTIVENESS OF OUR PRAYERS BY EMBRACING REVELATION AS AN INVITATION TO PRAY.

" . . . our prayers *from* earth are instrumental in releasing heaven's power *to* earth. Many prayers have been received and preserved until God determines the appropriate time of their fulfillment." (Pg. 68, Paragraph 4)

Share with others a time when the answer to a prayer was delayed. Include what your experience was like and how it was resolved in your own heart.

Are there things you have given up praying for because you believed God was not listening or because you saw no answer?

Do you feel a new hope to begin praying for them again?

What types of things might God call us to pray for over a long period of time?

Personally:

In Nations:

PRAYER ACTION STEP

ON YOUR OWN...

Is there an area of your life that you know is out of harmony with the heart of God?

Take time to repent—giving it to God and seeking His intervention.

OR...

Begin again the process of praying for something you had put aside because you were disheartened about a delayed response.

Power To Pray

Study/Discussion Guide

"You would not have called to me unless I had been calling to you, said the Lion."

C.S. Lewis, The Silver Chair

Chapter Five
Authority to Pray for Nations

Quoting Don . . .
"We often confuse God's sovereignty (his ultimate authority over all things) with his rule (the active exercise of his authority)".

Pg. 74

Describe in your own words the difference between God's sovereignty and His rule.

According to Psalm 2:6-12 and Psalm 115:16, in whose authority does the "rulership" of the earth rest?

What implication does "your bearing authority on earth" have on your prayer?

I'm not sure we've given much thought to the difficulty God faced, and still faces.

Very simply love cannot be forced, it can only be offered.

Pg.75

Do you agree or disagree with this statement:

" . . . what this means is that without our prayer God will *not act*, God *must* be invited to bring his rule because we *want* it."

I agree because ...

I disagree because ...

Answering as honestly as possible, on a scale of 1 to 10 (if 1 is never and 10 is in all things), where would you place your own desire to see "God's will be done on earth as it is in heaven"? How would it change your life if His will always dictated your actions?

How do you think this might affect your commitment and passion to pray?

Jesus was made a man — so he could ask God as a man — for things on behalf of man. As a man he also invited God's mercy, presence and purpose for all mankind. Does this help you to feel able to connect to the ways he prayed? Why or why not?

In this short chapter, **"WHY PRAYER?"** what most impacted you, and in what ways?

PRAYER ACTION STEP

ON YOUR OWN...

Write out the Lord's Prayer. Personalize and expand it. As you write this, hold this picture in your mind . . . you and Jesus are praying this together.

Power To Pray

Study/Discussion Guide

"Everyone who acknowledges me publicly here on earth, I will also acknowledge before my Father in heaven."
Matthew 10:32

Chapter Six
Where Should We Pray?

> **It is not that all prayers must be public, it is that some prayer should be public.**
>
> **This is not just our simple idea, it is God's directive."**
>
> ***Pg. 82***

In what religions other than Christianity do people pray publicly?

Why do you think they pray in public?

How do we know what Jesus prayed?

Do you agree or disagree that public prayer is something that all disciples of Jesus are commissioned by God to participate in?

Why or why not?

Have you ever prayed out loud in a public place?

If yes, was the experience challenging or easy?

Why?

When you pray in public out loud, what attitudes do you feel are helpful to hold in the front of your mind?

Thinking of prayer as conversation with a person (God), read Luke 10:13–22. How would you describe the pattern of Jesus' conversation and prayer?

For further study of Jesus' pattern of public prayer look up the following Scripture verses:

John 11:32-44   Matt. 19:13-15
John 12:23-32   Matt. 27:45-50

PRAYER ACTION STEP

ON YOUR OWN . . .

Make plans with a friend or friends to go into a public place and pray . . . OR . . . purpose to look for a person who is unfamiliar to you who seems to need a touch from God. Offer to pray for them on the spot.

Note: The day I did this chapter I got a call from my sister. She lives in another state and was facing a medical procedure, which had her frightened, in tears, and dreading the pain that was to come. As she sat in the waiting room unable to stop crying, a middle-aged woman approached her and said: " I don't know what is wrong, but would you mind if I prayed for you?" My sister replied; "please do". There in the waiting room, surrounded by onlookers, the woman prayed. My sister was filled with God's peace and was able to stop crying. She went into the examining room – still feeling God's peace. After a preliminary test it was determined the painful procedure wasn't needed. My sister believes it was due to that woman's prayer and the grace of God.

Power To Pray

Study/Discussion Guide

"For the Lord is a faithful God. Blessed are those who wait for his help." Isaiah 30:18b

Chapter Seven
Our Prayer and the Helper

Think of this chapter with this subtitle, PARTNERING WITH THE HOLY SPIRIT IN PRAYER. Don and I have been "partners" for 44 years (2012), and we are pretty good at it. In fact we were chosen, along with several other couples, to play *The Newlywed Game* at a wedding party a couple of years ago. Each partner answers a series of questions while the other is out of the room. When the missing partner returns they have to guess how their mate would have answered the questions. We freaked out many people. Not only did we get all the answers correct, we used the exact same terminology to answer many of the questions. Why share this story here? It reminds me of what it's like to pray. We are here and God is in the other room . . . and somehow we need to know what to pray so he can answer. The Holy Spirit, who lives inside us, is the someone who knows his heart. However it's not so easy to catch what he is sometimes saying.

In spite of how well Don and I *"get"* each other, sometimes it's like we pass each other in the dark. Like today—I told him I wanted to go exploring around the town we were visiting on vacation. He thought I meant I wanted to drive around the lake. After he had passed all the side streets in town and we were approaching another town. I said, "What I really wanted to do was poke around in the town we were visiting—drive around the neighborhoods and the country roads of that town". "OHHH!" was his response as he turned the car around.

Communication that hits the mark is not so easy. Prayer is communication. It's an art not a science and it requires plenty of trial and error. I hope you find that encouraging. It is what this chapter is all about.

Define the word messenger.

"One of the practical results of receiving the Holy Spirit is that he becomes a supernatural partner with each of us in praying."
Pg. 89

Look up John 15:26, John 16: 7-8, 13-14. Whose messenger is the Holy Spirit?

Whose messenger are we called to be?

30

List some ways that our being God's messenger might relate to prayer.

Read Ephesians 6:10-20, and respond to the following questions.

Whom are we fighting?

Where do these powers exist?

Why might it be important to stay alert?

What types of weapons are required for our battle?

Are any of the weapons or pieces of armor things you can see with your eyes or feel with your hands?

What place does God's word play in partnering with the Spirit of God?

What percentage of our prayers is to be in partnership with the Holy Spirit?

What is God concerned that we pray about?

What does the success of Paul's message depend upon?

What does this imply about how partnering in prayer with the Holy Spirit affects the work of evangelism?

PARTNERING WITH THE HOLY SPIRIT

Here are three practical steps that will help you as you partner with the Holy Spirit in prayer. Make comments on what you find helpful or not helpful about each one.

1. Start Praying.

2. Listen for a voice behind you saying this is the right focus, (The Butterfly Anointing - Jack Hayford).

3. Pray according to the revelation you are given.

What is your experience of hearing the Holy Spirit as you pray?

Do you expect to hear his voice?

Instead of seeing revelation as the goal, we must see it as what it really is—the Coach sending in the play.
Pg. 91

How does hearing God's voice (getting impressions) — or not hearing His voice affect your prayers?

Have you had a memorable experience of feeling like your life's schedule was interrupted to ask you to pray for something or someone? Share that experience with others in your group.

How did you know it was God who was asking you to pray?

PRAYER ACTION STEP

ON YOUR OWN ...

Plan to spend 30 minutes on this exercise.
Find a quiet place where you can be alone. Quiet your heart and allow the Holy Spirit to direct whom to pray for. You will know who to apply the passage to because as you read the passage in your heart it will fit like a puzzle piece to its subject. Try praying out loud in a normal voice like you are having a conversation with God.

Look up Isaiah 30 and read through it so it becomes familiar. Then re-read it and listen for the voice of the Holy Spirit and allow him to direct your prayer as if the passage were one piece of a puzzle that fit perfectly into one of the four puzzle pieces mentioned below. Let your heart rest on only one of the subjects, disregarding the other three. Don't feel you need to pray the entire chapter (not all of it will fit, just choose the portions that stand out to you). Don't be afraid to employ Jack Hayford's "Butterfly Anointing".

For your personal life ... **OR**

For the life of the Church of Jesus ... **OR**

For the life of someone you love ... **OR**

For the life of your nation.

Power To Pray

Study/Discussion Guide

The earnest prayer of a righteous man produces wonderful results. James 5:16

Chapter Eight
The Rule of Wrestling

Describe what you believe distinguishes "earnest" prayer from "ineffective" prayer?

Read Mark 9:14-29. From this story and Jesus' final comment to his disciples (v.29), what rule or principle you could write about prayer?

What can we do to increase God's presence, power and authority in our lives?

Illustrate below, using a mathematical equation, the principle of prayer found in James 5:16b.

"Ministry engages people on God's behalf.

Prayer engages God on behalf of people."
   Pg. 100

Mark on the scale below the spirit of your own prayers (aiming for an average).

Passionless 1 2 3 4 5 6 7 8 9 10 Earnest

What themes are you are most likely to pray earnestly for?

> *"God reveals so that we may know how to live a life of faith."*
> *Pg. 103*

Re-write in your own words Habakkuk 2:4 NLT

What does it mean to live by faithfulness to God? Romans 1:17

> *"The secret things belong to the Lord our God, but the things revealed belong to us and to our sons forever..."*
> *Deut. 29:29*

Do you live as though your life with God is made right by faith alone?

Why do you need faith in your own heart to stand before God and pray?

> *"What it means to live a life of faith is to discover what God has revealed about himself and then live our lives as if that were in fact true."*
> **Pg. 103**

Do you think of prayer as entering into a wrestling match with God?

How might this change your expectations regarding prayer?

THE LAW OF WRESTLING

1. *Wrestling for God's Presence*
   *All effective pray-ers have come to realize that any blessing without His presence is empty. They have come to realize that in prayer we are wrestling not for a blessing of God but for the God who brings blessings. We need him to come with it. Every request that is **of** God is **for** God."* Pg. 109

Try honestly to think about your prayers for God's intervention. Is getting more of God's presence what motivates your prayers?

When you've made His Presence the chief goal of your prayer, how has it influenced your prayer?

Share a challenging experience where you sought God's presence and it became the door of blessing in your situation?

2. *Wrestling With Who God Is*
   To wrestle effectively in prayer also means to wrestle with God—that is to wrestle with who God is. Pg.109

Read Hebrews 4:16. According to this passage what action must we take to encounter God in prayer?

How might our imagination play a helpful role in effectively doing this?

The point is that wrestling in prayer is to argue with God for an outcome based on his character and his revealed will and promises. God is looking for active partners not passive watchers.
Pg. 111

Do you find it easy, helpful or difficult to visualize yourself before God when you pray?

Why?

Does the idea of arguing with God make you uncomfortable or seem disrespectful?

Does a God who invites you to dialogue/argue about how he should act, change most of your view of prayer—your view of God, or your view of yourself?

Explain:

Look up Acts 9:36-42. As you read this story use your imagination to put yourself in the story. Based on what is said to Peter (if you had been there as a silent observer) when Peter knelt down to pray, write what his prayer might have sounded like. Be sure to take time to share your version of his prayer with one another.

Read Exodus 32:1-14. Share your reflections of this passage with your group.

Do you believe your prayers can change God's mind?

3. <u>Wrestling With God Through Fasting</u>
   "... fasting is not some seldom-mentioned reserved–for–only–spiritual–giants kind of activity. It is presented in both the Old and New Testaments as a normal part of wrestling in prayer." Pg. 113

Read Deuteronomy 8:3.
What two things was God aiming for when he required people to fast?

   1.

   2.

Why might these things still be important for us today?

Do you find fasting a helpful tool for humbling yourself and creating dependency on God alone?

Why or why not?

4. <u>Wrestling with God Requires Persisting in Prayer.</u>
"*I will not let you go unless you bless me.*"
Genesis 32:26
"*An inheritance gained hurriedly at the beginning will not be blessed in the end.*"
Proverbs 20:21

Who is God's inheritance?

How long will he wrestle for it?

Who is our inheritance?

Try to think of some reasons why we should do less wrestling than God?

What are two points Don makes about the need to be persistent in our prayers?
                                Pp. 115-117

    1.

    2.

Do you find it easy or hard to persist in unanswered prayer?

Why?

PRAYER ACTION STEP

ON YOUR OWN...

Done on your own — unless you have a medical condition that prevents you from doing so — plan a 24 hour fast this week.
The Jewish way of fasting is from sunset of one day to sunset of the next. That means beginning your fast with dinner on one day and ending it by eating dinner the next day. You may find this method helpful. Increasing your water intake is helpful so that you don't become dehydrated.

Here are some spiritual exercises to choose from during your fast if you cannot come up with one of your own.

> TAKE A PRAYER WALK
>
> WRITE A LETTER TO GOD
>
> PRAY THROUGH PSALM 37

Power To Pray

Study/Discussion Guide

"He is seated on the throne in anticipation of our appearance." Don Anderson

Chapter Nine
The Throne of the Lamb

Begin by sharing a story of when your prayer seemingly changed an outcome.

Read Hebrews 14:16. What words might you use in place of "coming boldly" and "throne of grace"?

Why, when praying, do we spiritually stand before God's throne?

Rewrite in your own words:
Colossians 3:1-3

"Prayer... is God's arrangement for safe power sharing with us in his intention to bless the world through us."

Dallas Willard

Philippians 1:27

> *"The Bible never attaches prayer to coincidences; it will always attach them to consequences."*
> **Pg. 120**

Ephesians 2:6

What is the one and only thing that qualifies a person to stand before God and pray?

Read Revelation 5:8. Picture the scene! Where are our prayers stored and what are they doing?

When might be the only time they leave the throne room?

As you consider how long your prayers may remain with God, in what manner would you like the voice of your prayer to continue to cry out to him?

How Do We Pray "In Jesus Name"?

"I tell you the truth, anyone who believes in me will do the same works I have done, and even greater works, because I am going to be with the Father. You can ask for anything in my name, and I will do it, so that the Son can bring glory to the Father. Yes, ask me for anything <u>in my name,</u> and I will do it!" John 14:12-14

1. *We pray "In Jesus' Name" when we pray things that glorify the name of Jesus. He will then in turn be free and delighted to glorify the Father by answering our prayer.*

   "Our task is to pray for things that will increase and extend the honor of his name; the power sharing of God will always have this purpose." (Pg. 125) What percentage of your prayers has this as their goal?

   "By living lives and praying prayers continually aimed at bringing glory to the name of Jesus Christ, we will be continually increasing in our boldness and authority in every prayer".
   Pg. 125

   If you began to intentionally have this as a goal, how would it change the way you pray?

2. *We pray "In Jesus' Name" when we pray according to the revealed meaning of Jesus name.*

Review Matthew 1:20-23. What did the angel of God say were the two revealed meanings of the name Jesus. (Remember that to God, a name reveals function and destiny).

The Greek word for the Holy Spirit in John 15:26 is Paraclete.

It holds within it the meanings Advocate, Helper, Comforter, Encourager, Counselor.

What is the body and aim of prayers that reveal the name of Jesus as God with us?

Do you find yourself consistently praying for things that relate to these two desires of God's heart?

Read John 15:26 through John 16:15 In this passage Jesus identifies the name and job description of the Holy Spirit. Remember to God names reveal function and destiny. List the specifics of his job description.

What other passages can you think of that describe the work of the Holy Spirit?

When you think about Jesus leaving earth so that he could send us the Holy Spirit to live within us always, (he is as present now as Jesus was present when he lived on earth in the flesh) how do you feel?

3. *We pray "In Jesus' Name" when we pray for God's purposes to be fulfilled according to the heart of Jesus. His heart and actions proclaim that mercy triumphs over judgment.*

Do you find it easier to pray for mercy or for judgment?

Why?

What are particular issues that offend you to the point of a self- awareness—where it is almost impossible for you to have God's heart of mercy?

Why?

Does it relate to a specific hurt you have experienced where you may need to do further forgiving?

Revelation 5:9-10
"And they sang a new song with these words, 'You are worthy to take the scroll and break its seals and open it. For you were slaughtered, and your blood has ransomed people for God from every tribe and language and people and nation. And you have caused them to become a kingdom of priests for our God. And they will reign on the earth.'"

According to Revelation 5:9-10, what two things does Jesus do that reveal his heart for man?

What does this say about Jesus' relationship to God the Father?

What would you say is Jesus' gift to His Father?

Chapter 1 of *Power to Pray* is titled, "Our Name is House of Prayer". It began with the story of Jesus overturning the tables of moneychangers and driving them from the temple—proclaiming "My Father's house shall be called a House of Prayer for all the Nations" (Mark 11:15). In this act he reveals our name and our destiny.

In Chapter 8 titled, "The Rule of Wrestling", we reviewed Jesus pre-incarnate encounter with Jacob. Here Jacob wrestles with Jesus for a blessing. Jesus blesses him by giving him a new name—Israel—"because you wrestled with God and man and won." The blessing Jesus gives is an ongoing job. We saw that Israel has a two-fold meaning—God wrestles in man and Israel wrestles with God for a blessing.
Gen. 32:22-28.

In this current chapter titled, "Throne Room of the Lamb" we conclude with Revelation 5:9-10. This revelation happens as we are approaching the end of time, as we know it.

Understand that God and Heaven are outside of time, and not confined to our space-time parameters. Here a new song is sung in heaven to Jesus. It declares who he is and what he has done!

When you think about the story line of these passages, what was Jesus always engaged in and what has been his forever goal for you?

Is he going to be successful?

PRAYER ACTION STEP

ON YOUR OWN...

Take time to review your notes on this chapter. As you think about "coming boldly before the Throne of Grace and you consider what it means to pray in the Name of Jesus, let the Holy Spirit rest on any area where you may need a heart change. God never overwhelms us with guilt — that is the work of the accuser. Rather he opens our eyes to see things in new ways and with his own compassion he invites us to trust him as one with mercy and power to bring change.

Respond to the voice of the Holy Spirit by writing a prayer. See yourself presenting it to God in the Throne Room of the Lamb.

OR

Spend some time writing your own song or prayer of praise and worship glorifying and thanking the Lamb who was slain and who purchased with his blood a nation of priests, among whom you stand.

Power To Pray

Study/Discussion Guide

"Truth cannot be defeated."
Edwin Louis Cole

Chapter Ten
Praying That Works

> *"The words of God are words God in heaven longs to fulfill. He waits only for his partners on earth to ask."*
> Pg. 140

In the first sentence of this chapter Don uses the word "tool" to describe God's word. Write down all the characteristics you can think of that describe a good tool.

When in a discussion with another, and they use your own words as evidence to make their point, how do you feel?

Children, spouses and parents are particularly gifted with the ability to remember what you once said. Why do you think this is true?

54

What might be some of the reasons behind the misuse of God's word in prayer?

How do you expect God to deal with prayers based on a misuse of his word?

> "...The word of God is truth and has the power of truth —when aimed correctly. It's not a toy gun, and it's not a fake gun."
> Pg. 132

MEMORIZE JEREMIAH 23:29

"Does not my word burn like fire?" says the Lord. Is it not like a mighty hammer that smashes a rock to pieces?"

AND . . . ISAIAH 55:10-11

"The rain and snow come down from the heavens and stay on the ground to water the earth. They cause grain to grow, producing seed for the farmer and bread for the hungry. It is the same with my word. I send it out, and it always produces fruit. It will accomplish all I want it to and will prosper everywhere I send it."

Here are some reasons that Jesus (our model) depended upon God's Word:

1. God's Word has power because it is true. (Proverbs 30:5)

2. It is God's truth revealed specifically to us — so that we might apply it to life. (Matt. 4:4, Luke 4:4, Deut. 8:3)

3. It is living and powerful. (Heb.4:12, 11:3, Jeremiah 23:29, Isaiah 55:10-11)

4. It conveys the will of God. (Psalm 119)

5. We live in the midst of a "spiritual" battle and God's Word is the (our) "spiritual" offensive weapon crafted and forged by God himself for our joint victory over the enemy. (Eph. 6:13-17)

Which of the above reasons motivate you the most and why?

Rate yourself on the scale of 1 to 10 below with 1 being "I seldom pray God's Word, and 10 being "I regularly pray God's Word".

1 2 3 4 5 6 7 8 9 10

What would you commit to do to move up the scale a notch or two over the next two months?

In conclusion, what chapters from Don's book, Power to Pray, most changed your view of prayer?

Why?

If you are doing this book within the context of a group, take time to share your answers with one another.

Pray for one another in the areas you would each like to experience change in your prayer life.

PRAYER ACTION STEP

ON YOUR OWN...

Using Don's model of praying a passage of scripture, choose a favorite Psalm and pray it this week.

If you don't have a favorite Psalm here are some of my favorites.

Psalm 103

Psalm 91

Psalm 126

Psalm 127

Psalm 29

Psalm 1

Psalm 92

Psalm 146

Psalm 23

Made in the USA
Charleston, SC
06 September 2013